THIS LAND CALLED AMERICA: **ALABAMA**

CREATIVE EDUCATION

Published by Creative Education
P.O. Box 227, Mankato, Minnesota 56002
Creative Education is an imprint of The Creative Company
www.thecreativecompany.us

Book and cover design by Blue Design (www.bluedes.com)
Art direction by Rita Marshall
Printed in the United States of America

Photographs by Alamy (John Elk III, fi online, Ladi Kirn), Corbis (William
A. Blake, Michael Callan; Frank Lane Picture Agency, Philip Gould,
Bob Sacha), Getty Images (After Charles Bird King, Don Cravens/
Time & Life Pictures, Digital Vision, Robert Francis, Derek Henthorn,
Fred Hirschmann, Hulton Archive, Andrew Kornylak, Erik S. Lesser,
David McLain/Aurora, MPI, National Geographic, Louis Requena, H.
Armstrong Roberts/Retrofile, Harrison Schull, Jerry Young)

Library of Congress Cataloging-in-Publication Data
Shofner, Shawndra.
Alabama / by Shawndra Shofner.
p. cm. — (This land called America)
Includes bibliographical references and index.
ISBN 978-1-58341-626-6
1. Alabama—Juvenile literature. I. Title. II. Series.
F326.S57 2007
976.1—dc22   2007006954

First Edition
9 8 7 6 5 4 3 2 1

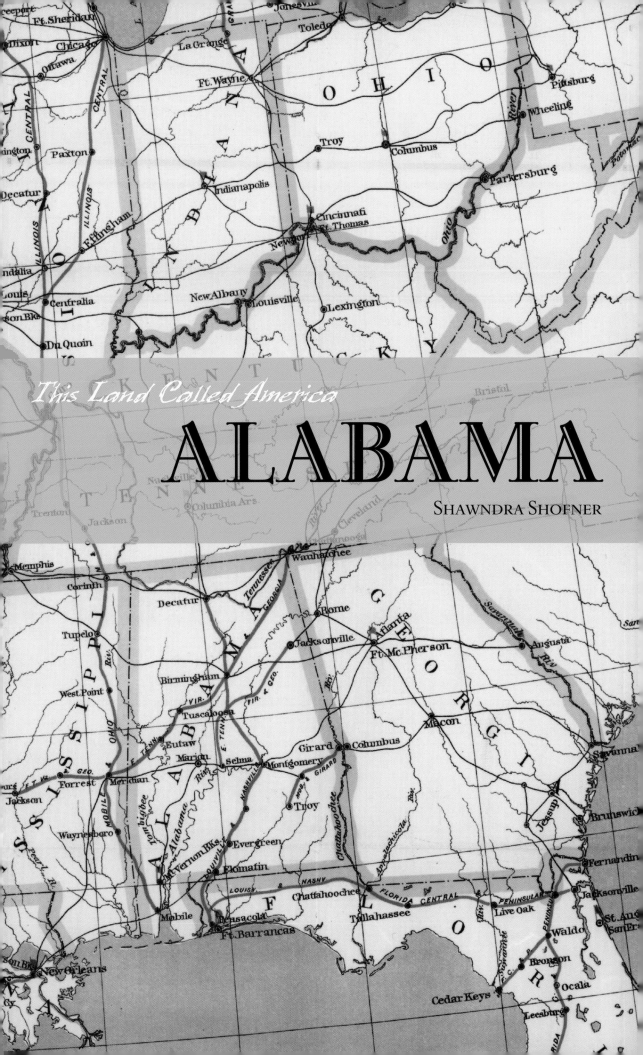

This Land Called America

ALABAMA

SHAWNDRA SHOFNER

Alabama

SHAWNDRA SHOFNER

IT IS DARK, JUST BEFORE THE SUMMER SUN RISES. GROUPS OF MEN, WOMEN, AND CHILDREN WAIT ON THE BEACH AT MOBILE BAY. THEIR LANTERNS AND FLASHLIGHTS SKIM ACROSS THE WATER. AS THE TIDE RISES, THE WATER BUBBLES WITH BLUE CRABS AND SHRIMP SWIMMING TOWARD SHORE. FLOUNDERS, CATFISH, STINGRAYS, AND EELS JOIN THEM. SOMEONE SHOUTS, "JUBILEE!" AND THE CROWD DASHES FORWARD WITH THEIR EMPTY COOLERS, PAILS, OR NETS. EVERYONE SCOOPS UP THE STRANDED FISH AND SHELLFISH. ON WARM SUMMER MORNINGS, PEOPLE IN ALABAMA TAKE PART IN JUBILEE, ONE OF THE MOST UNUSUAL SEAFOOD HARVESTS IN THE WORLD.

YEAR
1519 Spanish explorer Alonso Álvarez de Piñeda sails into Mobile Bay and explores Alabama's coast.
EVENT

Alabama Beginnings

Four major American Indian nations lived on, hunted in, and farmed the lands that would become the state of Alabama. These Indian nations were Creek, Choctaw, Chickasaw, and Cherokee. Alabama gets its name from a Creek tribe called the Alibamu. This tribe cleared trees and brush from the land and grew crops. The word *alibamu* means, "I clear the thicket."

A Creek chief

A Spanish explorer and mapmaker named Alonso Álvarez de Piñeda sailed along the Gulf Coast in 1519. He explored Alabama's Mobile Bay. After another explorer from Spain, Hernando de Soto, passed through Alabama in 1540, Spain claimed land north of the Gulf Coast, including present-day Alabama, as part of Spanish Florida.

King Charles II of England also owned part of the territory of modern Alabama. The land was part of the English province Carolina, which the king had given in 1663 to eight men who helped him regain the throne.

In 1677, French explorer René-Robert de La Salle sailed to

Creek Indians (above) originally lived throughout Alabama, including the area that is now Little River Canyon National Preserve (opposite).

YEAR

| 1540 | Spanish explorer Hernando de Soto clashes with Chief Tuskaloosa in the Battle of Maubila. |

EVENT

With the help of fort-builder Pierre Le Moyne, the Louisiana Territory became a safe place to live.

America. He claimed all of the land west of the Mississippi River to the Rocky Mountains and north from the Gulf of Mexico to Canada for France. He named the territory Louisiana after France's King Louis XIV. In 1702, French brothers Pierre and Jean-Baptiste Le Moyne founded Fort Louis de la Mobile near the Mobile River as the capital of the Louisiana Territory. France sold the territory, which included Alabama, to the

David Farragut

United States in the Louisiana Purchase of 1803. Alabama then became the 22nd U.S. state in December 1819.

Alabama was a cotton-farming state in the early 1800s. Cotton farmers in the American South relied on slave labor to produce the large amounts of the crop needed by other states and countries. Many people in northern states disagreed with the practice of slavery, though. They wanted all slaves to be set free. In an effort to hold on to their rights to own slaves, 11 Southern states, including Alabama, withdrew from the Union. The American Civil War between the North and South began in April 1861.

Northern admiral David Farragut took control of Alabama's Mobile Bay in 1864. His troops stopped supplies from getting to the Southern troops through the bay's port. The North eventually won the war in 1865, and Alabama was readmitted as a state in June 1868.

Alabamans worked to rebuild their lives and businesses after the war. Montgomery banker Josiah Morris helped form the Elyton Land Company in 1871 to mine for iron ore, coal, and limestone in north-central Alabama. These three

Admiral David Farragut retired from active duty because of poor health after the conflict at Mobile Bay.

YEAR

1703   French soldiers celebrate the first Mardi Gras in Mobile after recovering from yellow fever.

EVENT

- 9 -

Melted iron is mixed with recycled steel in a huge vat and put into a furnace to make new steel.

materials were then used to make steel. Soon, the new steel and iron industries, together with the existing Alabama and Chattanooga railroads, drew many workers, families, and other businesses to the area. They founded a city and named it Birmingham after the industrial city in England.

Even though steel and iron production was booming, many people in the state still owned or worked on cotton farms. In 1915, a tiny beetle called the boll weevil, which feeds on flowering cotton plants, destroyed much of Alabama's crop. Farmers switched to growing peanuts, sweet potatoes, and pecans. These crops were unaffected by the beetle. With new agricultural products and a booming steel industry, Alabama's economy grew rapidly in the 1900s.

At an iron-ore factory near Birmingham, Alabama, men made 200 tons (181 t) of iron per day in 1890.

1720   The capital of French Louisiana is moved from Mobile west to Biloxi, Mississippi.

In the Heart of Dixie

ALABAMA IS BORDERED BY FOUR STATES. TENNESSEE LIES TO THE NORTH. GEORGIA IS TO THE EAST. THE SOUTHERN BORDER IS FORMED BY FLORIDA AND THE GULF OF MEXICO. MISSISSIPPI BORDERS ALABAMA ON THE WEST.

Five land regions make up Alabama's geography. From south to north, they are the Gulf Coastal Plain, the Piedmont, the Appalachian Ridge and Valley, the Cumberland Plateau, and the Interior Low Plateau.

The Gulf Coastal Plain of Alabama sweeps across the southern two-thirds of the state. Land around Mobile is low and swampy. Higher land east of Mobile is used for farming. A gently sloping prairie of rich, black soil called the Black Belt runs through the middle of the plain. Hills covered with pine forests roll through the northern part of the Plain along Alabama's western border.

The Piedmont is north of the Gulf Coastal Plain. It starts at the Talladega Mountains in the center of the state and stretches east to the Georgia border. Alabama's highest point is near the city of Lineville, where Cheaha Mountain rises to 2,405 feet (733 m). Coal and iron ore mines, as well as limestone—a rock formed by shells and coral—and marble quarries, are found in the Piedmont area.

The Appalachian Ridge and Valley region lies north and west of the Piedmont. Sandstone ridges and fertile valleys are the main features of this region. Alabama's largest deposits of coal, iron ore, and limestone exist here—as do many industries, due to the easy access to such materials.

Alabama's Gulf Coast attracts shorebirds at sunset and vacationers along its beaches during the day.

YEAR

1721   The French ship *Africane* sails into Mobile harbor with 129 slaves from Guinea, West Africa.

EVENT

- 13 -

Northwest of the Ridge and Valley Region is the Cumberland Plateau. In the northern part of the Plateau, the Sandstone Highlands average an elevation of about 1,300 feet (396 m) above sea level. The Tennessee and Black Warrior rivers are main waterways that flow from the Ridge and Valley.

The Interior Low Plateau is located in the northwestern corner of the state. Its land is rich in limestone, but most of the land is used for farming cotton, corn, and hay. The area makes up part of the greater Tennessee River Valley.

There are no large natural lakes in Alabama. Any large lakes have been made by people as the result of electric-power

With its white beaches along the Gulf (above) and opportunities to climb in its river canyons (opposite), Alabama has plenty to offer outdoor enthusiasts.

France gives Alabama to England at the end of the French and Indian War.

dams on rivers. The Guntersville Dam on the Tennessee River created the largest lake in the state. Guntersville Lake is in northeastern Alabama. Its 110 square miles (285 sq km) stretch from Guntersville Dam to Nickajack Dam. Lakes Jordan, Mitchell, Lay, Logan Martin, Neely Henry, and Weiss were all created from dams on the Coosa River, which runs from northwestern Georgia south to Montgomery.

Rattlesnake

About two-thirds of Alabama's land is covered with forests. Bears, bobcats, and foxes make the wooded areas of oaks and maples their home. Deer, squirrels, rabbits, and wild turkeys are native to Alabama as well. Poisonous snakes such as rattlers, moccasins, and corals are common in the state's wilderness areas.

People in Alabama enjoy mild weather all year. Temperatures average around 80 °F (27 °C) in the summer with high humidity and are usually above 46 °F (8 °C) in the winter. About 56 inches (142 cm) of rain falls in the state every year. Most of the rain falls in the month of March. Northern Alabama sees snow occasionally, but warmer southern Alabama rarely gets snow.

Alabama's fertile farmlands (below) yielded 545,000 acres (220,554 ha) of cotton (opposite) in 2005.

The Cotton State

EXPLORERS FROM SPAIN WERE THE FIRST PEOPLE FROM EUROPE TO DISCOVER ALABAMA. BUT THEY DID NOT STAY LONG. FRENCH SOLDIERS FOUNDED ALABAMA'S FIRST CITY, MOBILE, IN 1702. SETTLERS SOON MOVED TO ALABAMA FROM VIRGINIA, NORTH AND SOUTH CAROLINA, GEORGIA, AND TENNESSEE. MOST WERE COTTON FARMERS. IMMIGRANTS FROM THE EUROPEAN COUNTRIES OF SPAIN, FRANCE, GREAT BRITAIN, ITALY,

Hank Aaron played 21
seasons for the Braves,
first in Milwaukee,
Wisconsin, then in
Atlanta, Georgia.

and Germany settled in Alabama in the late 1800s. Some set up rice, cotton, or vegetable farms. Others worked in the coal mines near Birmingham.

White farmers brought slaves from Africa to Alabama beginning in 1721. The slaves worked on large rice and cotton farms called plantations. By 1860, almost half of Alabama's population was made up of slaves, but by the Civil War's end in 1865, all of the slaves were set free. Still, African Americans were not treated like other free people. For almost 100 years more, they were forced to segregate, or separate, themselves from whites. They used separate rest rooms and drinking fountains, ate in separate restaurants, and sent their children to separate schools.

In 1934, future Major League Baseball star Hank Aaron was born in Mobile. Aaron held the record for most career home runs (755) until 2007. Although Alabama does not have any professional sports teams of its own, the state prizes athletes such as Aaron and Olympic runner Jesse Owens. Many Alabamans also cheer for the University of Alabama Crimson Tide football team.

The Civil Rights Movement started in Alabama in the 1950s. In December 1955, Rosa Parks, an African American

YEAR
1861   Alabama withdraws from the Union, and the capital of the South is established in Montgomery.
EVENT

1901   State lawmakers write up a constitution that restricts African Americans' ability to vote.

Rosa Parks (in the dark coat about to board the bus) later served on the staff of a Michigan congressman.

seamstress, was arrested in Montgomery for refusing to give up her bus seat to a white man. African Americans protested her arrest by refusing to ride a bus to go to work or shop for 382 days. The bus company and city businesses suffered great financial losses because of the boycott, and the peaceful demonstration brought national attention to the matter. In 1956, the Supreme Court ruled that segregation on public buses was unlawful.

On June 11, 1963, Alabama governor George Wallace blocked the entrance to the University of Alabama's Foster Auditorium to keep Vivian Malone and James Hood, two African Americans, from registering for classes. This incident is remembered as the "stand in the schoolhouse door." U.S. Attorney General Robert Kennedy (President John F. Kennedy's brother) sent in U.S. marshals to ensure that the students were allowed to enroll. Malone became the first African American to graduate from the university.

Recently, Alabama has welcomed a high number of immigrants from Laos, Vietnam, Cambodia, and China. Some mine for coal or work in Birmingham's steel factories. Others work at natural gas and petroleum wells in the southwestern counties of Mobile and Choctaw. Paper industries, lumber mills, and chemical manufacturers also employ many people.

Governor George Wallace (standing in the doorway) had run for office using the slogan "Segregation Forever."

YEAR
1955   Rosa Parks is arrested for refusing to give up her bus seat to a white passenger.
EVENT

- 23 -

Although there are many industries in Alabama, agriculture still leads the state's economy. Farmers grow at least 50 different crops, including cotton, peanuts, and watermelons. Businesses supporting Alabama's agricultural products employ about 21 percent of the state's workforce. They include farm equipment dealers, seed and feed suppliers, food processors, exporters, and retailers.

People stay in Alabama because of its opportunities for work, its mild year-round temperatures, and its beautiful places for recreation. In fact, Alabama has the highest retention rate out of all the states, in that more people who are born in Alabama continue to live there.

Apart from cotton, Alabama is also known for its peanut (above) and watermelon (opposite) crops, which grow well in different parts of the state.

Civil Rights leader Martin Luther King Jr. leads a protest march from Selma to Montgomery.

Amazing Alabama

EVERY YEAR SINCE 1703, A COLORFUL FESTIVAL CALLED
MARDI GRAS HAS BEEN HELD IN MOBILE, ALABAMA.
THE CELEBRATION LASTS FOR THREE WEEKS AND ENDS
THE DAY BEFORE ASH WEDNESDAY, A TRADITIONAL
CHRISTIAN DATE SIGNIFYING 46 DAYS BEFORE EASTER.
MORE THAN 24 PARADES MARCH THROUGH THE STREETS
OF MOBILE. PEOPLE DRESS UP IN CRAZY COSTUMES,

The city of Mobile is
known for its historic
houses (opposite) and
its Mardi Gras festivals.

decorate brilliant floats, toss beaded necklaces, and play instruments in marching bands.

Peanuts replaced cotton as the king crop in Alabama about 100 years ago. More than half of the peanuts grown in the U.S. come from farms within 100 miles (161 km) of Dothan, Alabama. This city is known as the "Peanut Capital of the World." The National Peanut Festival in Dothan honors peanut growers and peanuts. During the 10-day celebration in November, visitors can take in recipe contests and concerts. Children enjoy the amusement rides and circus acts.

Female boll weevils can deposit between 100 and 300 eggs in a cotton bud at one time.

Alabama is home to the world's only monument that honors a pest. The boll weevil monument, located in downtown Enterprise, is a statue of a woman holding a giant boll weevil over her head. The statue symbolizes Alabamans' ability to change and succeed, even when times are tough.

The largest cast-iron statue in the world overlooks Birmingham. Iron ore from this Alabama city was used to cast the 56-foot (17 m) Vulcan, the Roman god of fire, in 1904. The city made it for the World's Fair, which was held in St. Louis, Missouri, that year. The Statue of Liberty in New York City is the only statue in the U.S. larger than the Vulcan.

Natural wonders can be found throughout Alabama. The onyx and marble caves in northern Alabama's DeSoto Caverns

YEAR

1967   Lurleen Wallace becomes the first female governor in Alabama history.

EVENT

- 28 -

contain amazing stalagmites and stalactites. These are mineral deposits that form only in caves. In central Alabama's Eufaula National Wildlife Refuge, people can see protected animals such as the southern bald eagle, peregrine falcon, wood stork, and alligator. Southern Alabama offers beaches, Dauphin Island, and a crystal-clear, spring-fed swimming pool in Blue Spring State Park.

YEAR

1998   A massive tornado hits nine Birmingham suburbs, destroying more than 1,000 homes and businesses.

EVENT

- 29 -

QUICK FACTS

Population: 4,599,030

Largest city: Birmingham (pop. 236,620)

Capital: Montgomery

Entered the union: December 14, 1819

Nicknames: Heart of Dixie, Cotton State, Yellowhammer State

State flower: camellia

State bird: yellowhammer

Size: 52,419 sq mi (135,765 sq km)—30th-biggest in U.S.

Major industries: agriculture, mining, steel-making

The First White House of the Confederacy is located in Ramer, a suburb of Montgomery, Alabama. In 1861, the mansion's owner, Colonel Edmund Harrison, rented it to the Southern states' president, Jefferson Davis. Davis and his wife hosted many parties and receptions there.

In the small town of Tuscumbia in northwestern Alabama, people can tour the home of Helen Keller. Keller was born in 1880 and suffered a disease while still a baby that left her deaf and blind. The grounds contain the famous water pump where she learned that the liquid from the pump and the letters w-a-t-e-r her teacher spelled on her palm meant the same thing.

Racing fans trek to Talladega Super Speedway each May to watch the Winston 5000 NASCAR Cup Race. They can also visit the adjoining International Motorsports Hall of Fame and Museum. There, people can see race cars and memorabilia from 1902 to the present day.

As Alabama's population continues to grow, so do its business interests in car manufacturing and technology. Yet, while they are making room for the future, citizens are also working hard to preserve Alabama's historic past and maintain its natural areas. Alabamans want to keep their state in its characteristically amazing shape for many years to come.

YEAR

2006 A school bus is hit by a car and rolls off a bridge in Huntsville, injuring 23 and killing 4.

EVENT

BIBLIOGRAPHY

Alabama Archaeology. "Prehistoric Alabama." The University of Alabama. http://bama.ua.edu/~alaarch/ prehistoricalabama/paleoindian.htm.

Bockenhauer, Mark H., and Stephen F. Cunha. *National Geographic: Our Fifty States.* Washington: National Geographic, 2004.

Carpenter, Allan. *Alabama.* Chicago: Children's Press, 1978.

Everything Alabama. "Alabamiana: A Guide to Alabama." Alabama Live. http://www.al.com/alabamiana/index .ssf?facts.html.

Fradin, Dennis. *Alabama in Words and Pictures.* Chicago: Children's Press, 1980.

Marsh, Carole, and Kathy Zimmer. *Let's Discover Alabama.* Atlanta: Gallopade International, 2001.

INDEX